PRESIDEN.... .. ..

The Very Curious Language of George W. Bush

Volume 3

Edited by
Robert S. Brown

Foreword by
John Brady Kiesling

★ ★ ★ ★

Outland Communications, LLC
Skaneateles, New York

For information about discount purchases or purchasing Outland's George W. Bush (Mis)Speak
Desk Calendars, please contact Outland Books at (315) 685-8723 or www.outlandbooks.com

Published by Outland Books
Outland Communications, LLC
P.O. Box 534
25 Hannum Street
Skaneateles, New York 13152

www.outlandbooks.com

ISBN: 0-9714102-9-1

Printed in the United States of America

This latest collection of Presidential (Mis)Speak is dedicated to all those who have extended their support for this project and understood the broader significance of The Very Curious Language of George W. Bush.

"I'll talk about the values that make our country unique and different. We love freedom here in America."

George W. Bush

"Iraqis are sick of foreign people coming in their country and trying to destabilize their country, and we will help them rid Iraq of these killers."

George W. Bush

FOREWORD BY
John Brady Kiesling

*"...And so each venture
Is a new beginning, a raid on the inarticulate"*
— T.S. Eliot, East Coker

That such a work as Presidential (Mis) Speak should be necessary or even possible is a sad commentary on relations between the American people and their head of state in Washington. Part of the human condition is our frustration in finding the words to express or at least not betray the subtle and even noble thoughts of our better natures. We stumble through the compromises of our daily lives, using imprecise words that match the imprecision of our thoughts and feelings. And we accept that our communication will be imperfect, that the words we hear and use will be mangled or misplaced.

But we expect more from our politicians. We select them by an exhausting process that places all their strengths and weaknesses beneath the microscope of American public opinion. The electoral system has evolved, we think and hope, to identify and place at the service of the American people the individuals who correctly identify and express in well-chosen word and noble deed the highest aspirations of the nation. Failing that, we look for someone who will defend our interests. Failing that, we settle for someone who looks and sounds "presidential" to be the face and voice of America to the world.

Something has gone wrong with the electoral process when one outcome of it is Volume Three of the current series. This new volume of the malapropisms of George W. Bush, collected by Robert S. Brown, offers chilling insights into the character of the man who functions as our 43rd President. All of us acquire by early adulthood a vocabulary of words and phrases, the building blocks of the conventional wisdom of our tribe. It is of course forgivable when a president, like lesser mortals, fumbles in the articulation of a complex argument. But this president, whether out of intellectual laziness, or profound incuriosity, or some deeper psychopathology, cannot reliably parrot even the most basic management school slogans that—along with his family connections—won him his foothold in Texas business and politics.

Remember that the President has around him a team of expert speechwriters and political consultants, whose every waking moment is dedicated to arming him with the words and sentiments best suited to his situation. Perhaps these men accurately assess the educational limitations of the American people in giving their president a fifth-grade vocabulary. But they too have seen him stumble catastrophically over words that every politically aware American must cope with. And not every moment in a president's life can be scripted.

Americans presumably elect the leaders they want and deserve. If we wanted a leader like Prime Minister Tony Blair of Great Britain, someone with a reasoned and eloquent argument for every occasion, we could have found one. Political discourse is not dead in this country. But too many of us thought, in November of 2000, that words and the ideas behind them are less important than the "character" we pretend to be able to read in a candidate's face and posture. We have now the benefit of four years of hindsight. Each of us can judge: Am I—is America—stronger or richer or safer or better or more just or more democratic or more free than four years ago?

I had the privilege of serving four American presidents overseas during my twenty years as a Foreign Service Officer. I was a professional, representing America's official policy and not my personal political preferences. I resigned because this President and his policies had blackened America's image in the eyes of the world to make our country and people less safe. The planet is not in a popularity contest, and America's image must sometimes take a beating when we exercise the global responsibilities that come with being a superpower. But no president of the United States has inspired such contempt and fear as this one, to so little purpose.

The President's inability to convey to the world America's values and goals is a grave loss to American security. Each smirk, each ill-chosen bit of bellicosity, drives another nail in the coffin of the greatest alliance this world has ever known. Washington was once the "capital of the free world." Few outside this country would say that now with a straight face.

This Administration prides itself on being "faith-based." Let us demand some basic consistency. "In the beginning was the word" is not a bad starting point. The American system is based on the belief that words matter: freedom, equality, democracy, justice, security and peace are not campaign slogans or a mantra to be mindlessly repeated, but the fundamental organizing ideas of American society. The American people have the right to demand from their leaders a full and nuanced understanding of these terms. President George W. Bush pledged America's sacred honor in the name of "liberty" and "democracy," but in Iraq, Afghanistan and elsewhere, those words have become a tattered fig leaf for a failed policy.

I was honored to provide this introduction to Robert S. Brown's latest "raid on the inarticulate." In this election year, I hope the work in your hands will be read not as another cheap attack on the well-known limitations of a rather limited politician, but rather as a small contribution to the next new beginning of an America in which words keep their meaning.

John Brady Kiesling
Former U.S. Foreign Service Officer *

*Editor's Note: I am grateful to Mr. Kiesling for kindly taking the time to provide his thoughts for this latest collection of (Mis)Speak. For those unaware, it should be noted that John Brady Kiesling, at great personal cost, resigned in protest his position as a career Foreign Service Officer just prior to the U.S.-led invasion of Iraq. To read his profoundly eloquent and widely publicized letter of resignation addressed to Secretary of State Colin Powell, go to www.outlandbooks.com/kiesling

Mr. Kiesling is currently a Visiting Associate Professor at Princeton University's Woodrow Wilson School of Public and International Affairs.

"The world is more peaceful and more free under my leadership."

George W. Bush

PRESIDENTIAL SPEAK

"The servants of this ideology seek tyranny in the Middle East and beyond… they seek to indeminate America into panic and retreat."

April 13, 2004 Reading from his teleprompter during a nationally televised address to the nation. Referring to terrorism. The White House, Washington, D.C.

"I'm sure there's a lot of people frightened—biotechnology is a long word and it sounds—they may say, well, I don't know if I'm smart enough to be in biotechnology, or it sounds too sophisticated to be in biotechnology."

November 7, 2003 *Too sophisticated indeed.* From a speech in Winston-Salem, North Carolina.

"Maybe between the time I left Camp David and here I'll learn more."

March 23, 2003 *Time travel all over the place.* Camp David, Maryland.

"It is dangerous in Iraq because there are some who believe that we're soft, that the will of the United States can be shaken by suiciders—and suiciders who are willing to drive up to a Red Cross center, a center of international help and aid and comfort, and just kill… The tactics to respond to more suiciders driving cars will alter on the ground."

October 28, 2003 *If the word sounds right, say it.* The White House, Washington, D.C.

PRESIDENTIAL SPEAK

"I'm proud of the sergeant. I'm proud to call him citizen. I'm proud to call him fellow citizen to America."

October 2, 2003 Making reference to Master Gunnery Sergeant Guadalupe Denogean who served in Iraq. White House, Washington, D.C.

★ ★ ★ ★

"There's what they call 'actionable intelligence,' to which our military has responded on a quick basis is improving."

December 15, 2003 Speaking in Washington, D.C.

★ ★ ★ ★

"The benefits of helping somebody is beneficial."

April 2000 *Can't argue with the logic.*

The Very Curious Language of George W. Bush™
Volume 3

PRESIDENTIAL SPEAK

"One of the great things about this country is a lot of people pray."

April 13, 2003 Washington, D.C.

"I want to thank you for what you're fixing to do, which is to man the grass roots, and to get on the phones, and get the signs out, and to turn out the vote."

November 10, 2003 Preparing to man the grass roots in Little Rock, Arkansas.

"I'm so pleased to be able to say hello to Bill Scranton. He's one of the great Pennsylvania political families."

September 15, 2003 *Bill Scranton - going it alone.* Drexel Hill, Pennsylvania.

"We marched to war. I don't if you remember, on your TV screens, last summer it—a year ago, summer—it said, 'March to War'. You turn on the TV, and there it says: 'March to War'. That's not a very conducive environment in which people are willing to take risk. It's not a positive thought. It's a necessary, in my judgment, obviously, to make America secure."

November 10, 2003 *'March to War'? – whatever gave those TV people that idea? Greer, South Carolina.*

"I think war is a dangerous place."

May 7, 2003 *Generally speaking, that would be one way of describing it. Washington, D.C.*

PRESIDENTIAL SPEAK

"Prime minister was a distinguished visitor of ours in Crawford, Texas, at our ranch. You might remember that I called him a man of steel. That's Texan for 'fair dinkum'."

October 23, 2003 Referring to Australian Prime Minister John Howard. Speaking to the press in Canberra, Australia.

"And the other lesson is that there are people who can't stand what America stands for, and desire to conflict great harm on the American people."

July 28, 2003 *Another classic malaprop.* Pittsburgh, Pennsylvania.

"I don't spend a lot of time thinking about... why I do things."

June 4, 2003 Speaking with the press onboard Air Force One.

"And finally, Mayor Al is with us—the mayor of Monroe. Al Cappuccilli is here. Thank you, mayor, for being with us. You must be filling the potholes, picking up the garbage. That's the way to go."

September 15, 2003 'Complimenting' the local mayor during a speech in Monroe, Michigan.

"We have faced challenge in this nation."

June 19, 2003 *This editor has faced challenge in this undertaking.* Fridley, Minnesota.

"I'll talk about the values that make our country unique and different. We love freedom here in America."

July 16, 2003 *Right, right, the only freedom-loving country in the world — America.* Speaking in Washington, D.C.

"And we live in an amazing world. And yet, in the midst of our world, there's a lot of folks who are dying and will die."

July 16, 2003 *And I don't intend to be one of those folks — not if I can help it — Editor.* Washington, D.C.

"We can help somebody who hurts by hugging a neighbor in need."

April 4, 2003 Camp Lejeune, North Carolina.

PRESIDENTIAL SPEAK

"Today when I landed I met a fellow named Roy Bubeck. You don't know Bubeck at all and I didn't either. Maybe some of you do."

October 3, 2003 *Referring to the CEO of the Badger Mutual Insurance Company — a man you may or may not know. Milwaukee, Wisconsin.*

★ ★ ★ ★

"I'm going to describe what we discussed a little earlier... We had a chance to visit with Teresa Nelson who's a parent, and a mom or a dad."

September 9, 2003 *Gender manipulation in Jacksonville, Florida.*

★ ★ ★ ★

"See, free nations do not develop weapons of mass destruction."

October 8, 2003 *They don't?* Washington, D.C.

"Education belongs to everybody. High standards belongs to everybody."

October 2, 2003 Right up to the White House, Washington, D.C.

"He told me he would put the budget of the Palestinian Authority on the Web page, and he did, which means he's a man of his word."

July 25, 2003 Summing up the Palestinian finance minister. White House, Washington, D.C.

PRESIDENTIAL SPEAK

"As you notice, when there's a hole in the ground and a person is able to crawl into it in a country the size of California, it means we're on a scavenger hunt for terror. And find these terrorists who hide in holes is to get people coming forth to describe the location of the hole, is to give clues and data. And we're on it."

December 15, 2003 *Fully on top of the situation.* Speaking in Washington, D.C.

"We need a energy policy."

June 19, 2003 *Granted, only one letter off… but still.* Fridley, Minnesota.

PRESIDENTIAL SPEAK

"The first part of your question is that–is whether or not the weapons of mass destruction question."

June 1, 2003 Dealing with questions in St. Petersburg, Russia.

"The true strength of America is the fact that we've got millions of fellow citizens who are willing to love a neighbor just like they would like to be loved themselves. That's the real strength of this country, because we're a deep and compassionate nation."

June 19, 2003 Feeling like a noncontributor to our "deep and compassionate nation" – I admit it, I just don't always "love" my neighbors. There was this one time, in fact, when... – Editor. Fridley, Minnesota.

PRESIDENTIAL SPEAK

"There's a lot of neighborliness taking place in the state of Virginia and North Carolina and Maryland, where if somebody hurts and somebody's lonely, somebody needs help is finding refuge and solace because a fellow citizen has taken it upon him or herself to help somebody in need."

September 22, 2003 Speaking at the Virginia State Police Academy. Richmond, Virginia.

"You and your wife have been a leader in education reform."

February 6, 2003 Morphing the Amir of Qatar and his wife into one during a visit to the Persian Gulf state.

"I want to thank all the other members of the Congress and the Senate who have joined us. Thank you all for taking time out of your busy schedules to share in this historic moment."

December 8, 2003 *Well, it's really "members of the House (of Representatives) and Senate"… but why quibble? Just letting our international readers know. Washington, D.C.*

"We want results in every single classroom so that one single child is left behind."

November 10, 2003 *Pity that poor child. Little Rock, Arkansas.*

PRESIDENTIAL SPEAK

"Today when I landed, I met a fellow named Irving Hall. Where are you, Irving? Right there—stand up. Now you can sit down. Irving Hall works for our government at the laboratories, the high tech—Sandia. I think you worked there, didn't you, Irving? Yes, he worked there. And came time to retire and his boss said, 'What are you going to do, Irving?' He said, 'Why don't you make a difference?'—I believe that's what your boss told me—what you told me your boss said. See, he met me at the airplane. I'd never met Irving before."

March 26, 2004 Curiouser and curiouser. Albuquerque, New Mexico.

"I believe, uh, that, uh—a marriage has served society well."

February 27, 2004 Referring to the issue of gay marriage. Washington, D.C.

"And in the new responsibility society, each of us is responsible for loving our neighbor just like we'd like to be loved ourself."

July 24, 2003 *I'm ashamed to say that I don't always live up to my 'responsibility', for which I have deep and unrelenting remorse. — Editor.* Dearborn, Michigan.

"I didn't mean to dis the New York Times editorial page, but I just didn't—I'm not reading it a lot these days."

December 12, 2003 Gettin' down with his homeys in Washington, D.C.

PRESIDENTIAL SPEAK

"People can read everything they want into it when they hear 'faith-based initiative'. That all of a sudden opens everybody's imagination in the world to vast possibilities, some which exist and some which don't."

July 16, 2003 *Living in a world of nonexistent possibilities. Washington, D.C.*

"And I'm glad Laura is here tonight. In my book, she's a fabulous first lady. And I love her a lot and I hope she loves me a lot for dragging her out of Texas."

July 18, 2003 *Should the Texas audience be insulted or flattered? Confusion in Dallas, Texas.*

"The voice of the people need to be heard..."

February 27, 2004 Speaking at the White House on the subject of gay marriage.

"My expectations in the Middle East are to call all the respective parties to their, uh, responsibility to achieve peace."

February 2, 2003 *Utterly clarifying the situation.* Speaking at the G8 Summit in Evian, France.

"The president and I talked about whether or not, you know, the ramifications of this initiative to Mexico."

January 12, 2004 *Not sure we do know.* Referring to US-Mexican immigration policies at the Summit of the Americas in Monterrey, Mexico.

PRESIDENTIAL SPEAK

"We're laying the groundwork for a national campaign—a national campaign that I believe will result in a great victory in November, 2002."

June 30, 2003 Back to the future in Tampa, Florida.

"I think the intelligent I get is darn good intelligence."

July 14, 2003 Responding to criticism of intelligence cited previously by the president while making a case for war against Iraq. *The intelligent wasn't so good after all.*

"It's important for the Georgian people to have a good and strong and peaceful relations with Russia."

February 25, 2004 Speaking to the press in the Oval Office during a visit to the White House by Georgian President Saakashvili.

PRESIDENTIAL SPEAK

"I want to thank the astronauts who are with us—the, uh, the courageous, uh, spacial entrepreneurs."

January 14, 2004 *Seeming a bit spacial himself.* Speaking at NASA Headquarters in Washington, D.C., on new U.S. space policy.

"I don't like the idea of having an undocumented economy in the greatest country in the face of the earth."

January 9, 2004 Speaking somewhere in the face of the earth.

"I wanna thank President Chirac's support in the latest resolution in the United Nations."

February 2, 2003 Extending a personal thank-you to French President Chirac's Support at the G8 Summit in Evian, France.

PRESIDENTIAL SPEAK

"I want to thank General John Fryer, the superintendent of schools here. I thought it was pretty interesting. When I was reading the background of the schools here, I see that you got you a general running the school system."

September 9, 2003 Jacksonville, Florida.

★ ★ ★ ★

"America's carry a heavy burden of taxes and debt that could slow consumer spending. I'm troubled by that."

January 7, 2003 *I'm troubled, too – Editor.* Speaking at the Economic Club in Chicago.

★ ★ ★ ★

PRESIDENTIAL SPEAK

"It's a windy day out there—which is a good day for a windy speaker."

January 7, 2003 Opening his speech to the Economic Club in Chicago.

★ ★ ★ ★

"She is a great first lady. I love her dearly. I'm proud to call her wife."

August 24, 2003 Speaking at a fundraiser in Portland, Oregon.

★ ★ ★ ★

"Since I was here, thanks to the bravery of our military and to friends and allies, the regime of Saddam Hussein is no more. The world is peaceful and free."

June 11, 2003 *Basking in the glow of an entire world now living in peaceful harmony due to the overthrow of Iraq's dictator.* Chicago, Illinois.

★ ★ ★ ★

PRESIDENTIAL SPEAK

"There have been no finer vice president of the United States than Dick Cheney. Mother may have a different opinion."

August 24, 2003 Speaking at a fundraiser in Portland, Oregon.

"I'm serving to steeze opportunities and that's what we're doin'."

August 24, 2003 *Fine.* Fundraiser. Portland, Oregon.

"First, let me make it very clear, poor people aren't necessarily killers. Just because you happen to be not rich doesn't mean you're willing to kill."

May 19, 2003 *Clearing up that uncertainty.* The White House, Washington, D.C.

PRESIDENTIALSPEAK

"We have differences, in the past."

February 27, 2004 Showing the usual disregard for verb tense while referring to German Chancellor Gerhardt Schroeder during the German leader's visit to the White House.

★ ★ ★ ★

"We are a country of law."

January 12, 2004 Speaking to the press in Monterrey, Mexico. Summit of the Americas.

★ ★ ★ ★

"The vice president and I went fishing. We threw our first lure at about 6:20 a.m. this morning. Looks like—turns out the fish like cooler weather than hot weather. Probably the press corps feels the same way. Turns out this is our hundredth day since major military operations have ended, ended in Iraq."

August 8, 2003 Interesting segué in Crawford, Texas.

"I was pleased to hear that many of the airports up east are beginning to have flights leave and that's good."

August 15, 2003 Speaking down west in San Diego, California, about the power outage that affected the Northeast U.S. and Canada.

"All of us is sorry that fire has devastated life and the countryside here."

August 11, 2003 *All of us is sorry too – Editor.* Summerhaven, Arizona.

"I want to thank the people for Summerhaven for allowing us to come up to visit your beautiful part of the world."

August 11, 2003 Thanking the people for Summerhaven, Arizona.

PRESIDENTIAL☜SPEAK

"A good education system is one that is going to mean more likely for any country, including ourselves, to be a freer country, and a more democratic country. And [Pakistan's President Musharraf] is—he's taking on the issue in a way that is a visionary and strong."

June 24, 2003 Camp David, Maryland.

"I have found the president to be an easy man to talk to. He expresses opinions very clearly and it's easy to understand."

May 14, 2003 Feeling at ease with South Korean President Roh Moo Hyun. Washington, D.C.

PRESIDENTIAL SPEAK

"By making the right choices, we can make the right choice for our future."

July 16, 2003 *Right, right, the only freedom-loving country in the world — America.* Speaking in Washington, D.C.

"By mentoring a child, you shape the character of a child. And it's a high calling in life because that influence reaches to eternity."

October 29, 2003 *I honestly won't dispute that — Editor.* Dallas, Texas.

"And we base it—our history and our decision making, our future— on solid values. The first value is, we're all God's children."

July 16, 2003 Separating church from state in Washington, D.C.

The Very Curious Language of George W. Bush™
Volume 3

PRESIDENTIAL SPEAK

"Any skeptic about what I'm talkin' about oughta come and talk to the people who know what they're talkin' about."

August 11, 2003 *Now you're talkin'.* Promoting governmental policy intended to promote "Healthy Forests". Summerhaven, Arizona.

"There's no bigger task than protecting the homeland of our country."

August 23, 2002 *Feeling safe and sound – deep in the homeland of our country – Editor.* Stockton, California.

"Uh, I think that, uh, one of the greatest contributions to Poland to our country is Polish Americans."

January 14, 2003 Responding to a Polish reporter in the Oval Office during a press conference with Polish President Kwasniewski.

The Very Curious Language of George W. Bush™
Volume 3

PRESIDENTIAL SPEAK

"See, without the tax relief package, there would have been a deficit, but there wouldn't have been the comm—commiserate—the, the, the, the—not commiserate—the, the, the—kick to our economy that occurred as a result of the tax relief."

December 15, 2003 *No, not commiserate.* Washington, D.C.

"Delays in our courts prevent us from doing the job necessary to maintain a healthy forests."

August 11, 2003 Continuing his estrangement from the world of tense agreement in Summerhaven, Arizona.

PRESIDENTIAL SPEAK

"I wanna remind you all that I—in, in order—what in order to fight and win the war it requires a expenditure of money that is commiserate with keeping a promise to our troops to make sure that they're well-paid, well-trained, well-equipped."

December 15, 2003 *Commensurating with the press.* Washington, D.C.

"I really appreciate the hardworking staff—the docs, the nurses, the people who make this fantastic facility operate in a way that makes me pride."

December 18, 2003 *I'd be pride too – Editor.* Washington, D.C.

PRESIDENTIALSPEAK

"I've got very good relations with President Mubarak and Crown Prince Abdullah and the King of Jordan—Gulf Coast countries."

May 29, 2003 Showing off a mastery of geography.

★ ★ ★ ★

"Security is the essential roadblock to achieving the road map to peace."

July 25, 2003 Hoping to achieve the road map to peace in the Middle East. Washington, D.C.

★ ★ ★ ★

"Today, Iraqis are liberated people. The former regime is gone, and our nation and the world is more secure."

August 14, 2003 Speaking at Marine Corps Air Station, Miramar, California.

The Very Curious Language of George W. Bush™
Volume 3

PRESIDENTIAL SPEAK

"I'm sorry my neighbor, his eminence Theodore Cardinal McCarrick, is not with us. He's a decent man. I'm really, really am proud to call him friend. He's a really good guy, as we say in Texas."

January 9, 2004 Speaking to the Catholic Educational Association, as they say in Texas. Washington, D.C.

★ ★ ★ ★

"Now, al-Qaida's still active, and they're still recruiting, and they're still a threat because we won't cower."

August 14, 2003 Addressing marines and sailors at the Marine Corps Air Station in Miramar, California.

★ ★ ★ ★

PRESIDENTIAL SPEAK

"The cooperation that we've achieved between our two countries? You've just articulated, uh, uh, that level of, uh, cooperation a way that I don't think I ever could."

January 12, 2004 Referring to Mexican President Fox's description of US - Mexican relations. Speaking with self-awareness in Monterrey, Mexico, at the Summit of the Americas.

"I think, you know, one of the things we'll have to do, of course, is take an assessment of why the cascade was so significant—why it was able to ripple so significantly throughout our system up east."

August 14, 2003 Speaking from back west in San Diego, California.

"When you're going to your coffee shops and your community centers that say, 'what is George W. up to?', you tell them this: that I'm doing the people's business in Washington, D.C."

January 15, 2004 Speaking at a 'Bush-Cheney 2004' reception in Atlanta, Georgia. From White House transcript.

"When I picked the secretary of education I wanted somebody who knew something about public education."

April 30, 2003 *Makes sense.* Referring to Rod Paige, U.S. Secretary of Education, at a White House ceremony.

"I've asked Congress to fund $100 million for the Compassionate Capital Fund. That's a fancy word for providing money for organizations like the Urban League to teach some of these small faith programs how to apply for grants, how to help manage and train their staffs."

July 28, 2003 *Using fancy word(s).* Pittsburg, Pennsylvania.

"When I picked the secretary of education… I wasn't interested in a theorists."

April 30, 2003 Referring to Secretary of Education Rod Paige at a White House ceremony honoring the Teacher of the Year.

PRESIDENTIAL SPEAK

"She is a fabulous first lady. I was a lucky man when she said, 'Yes, I agree to marry you.' I love her dearly, and I'm proud of the job she's doing on behalf of all Americans. Just like I love my brother."

September 9, 2003 Jacksonville, Florida.

"Should Saddam Hussein seals his fate by refusing to disarm, by ignoring the opinion of the world, you'll be fighting not to conquer anybody, but to liberate people."

January 3, 2003 *"Opinion of the world"?* Speaking to troops at Fort Hood, Texas.

The Very Curious Language of George W. Bush™
Volume 3

PRESIDENTIAL SPEAK

"One thing that's happening that you need to know that will help us make the necessary calculations for troop levels is that there's a lot of Iraqis beginning to be trained to deal with the issue on the ground. There's Iraqis being trained for an army. There's Iraqis being trained for an intelligence service. There's Iraqis being trained for additional police work… There's over 130,000 Iraqis now who have been trained, who are working for their own security."

November 20, 2003 *And there is a lot of Iraqis who could correctly renegotiate the use of verb tenses in the President's speech.* London, England.

"Everybody in Crawford says 'hello', starting with Laura. She is doing a fabulous day. I tell people it's because she's from Midland, Texas."

March 29, 2002 Speaking in Dallas, Texas.

"And we are making steadfast progress."

June 9, 2003 Speaking with the press after a cabinet meeting in the White House. Washington, D.C.

"Now, there are some who would like to rewrite history—revisionist historians is what I like to call them."

June 16, 2003 *What a coincidence — that's what I like to call them, too — Editor.* Elizabeth, New Jersey.

PRESIDENTIAL SPEAK

"Since September the 11th, the share of FBI resources dedicating to fighting terror has more than doubled."

September 9, 2003 Addressing FBI personnel at the FBI Academy in Quantico, Virginia.

★ ★ ★ ★

"I see a lot of the bubbas who work in my administration who've shown up."

December 12, 2003 Welcoming the 2003 NASCAR Winston Cup drivers to the White House.

★ ★ ★ ★

"I want to congratulate the Princeton womens and Coach Sailor for winnin' your sport back-to-back."

November 17, 2003 Greeting the NCAA national champion women's lacrosse team to the White House.

PRESIDENTIAL SPEAK

"The other thing that's necessary is to make sure we've got spending discipline in Washington. Is to make sure that Congress doesn't overspend. And that'll, ah,— because that'll affect the psychology of those who are risk capital in order to create the job base."

August 13, 2003 Crystal clear in Crawford, Texas.

"One thing I've learned, Karen, is not to negotiate with myself, particularly in front of cameras."

September 17, 2003 *Would be interesting to see, though.* Answering a question posed by a Reuters News Service reporter at the White House.

PRESIDENTIAL SPEAK

"As members of the press corps here know, I have at times complained about leaks of security information, whether the leaks be in the legislative branch or in the executive branch. And I take those leaks very seriously. … I'd like to know who leaked, and if anybody has got any information inside our government or outside our government who leaked, you ought to take it to the Justice Department so we can find out the leaker."

October 6, 2003 *Routing out the leakers.* Speaking in Washington, D.C.

★ ★ ★ ★

PRESIDENTIAL💬SPEAK

"There's no cave deep enough for America, or dark enough to hide."

August 29, 2002 Speaking in Oklahoma City.

"The more people involved in Iraq, the better off we will be. And that's exactly what our intention is, to encourage people to participate in the—making Iraq more secure and more free. A free Iraq is a crucial part of winning the war on terror. And now I'm going to go see to it that the prime minister is well-fed. We're going to feed him some chicken."

July 21, 2003 Getting down to the real business of feeding Italian Prime Minister Silvio Berlusconi in Crawford, Texas.

PRESIDENTIAL SPEAK

"America's a fabulous country, fabulous not only because of the values we hold dear but fabulous because of the nature of the people, who the American people."

August 22, 2003 Waxing eloquent at the Ice Harbor Lock and Dam in Burbank, Washington.

"These are the students who sometimes in the public school system are, uh, are deemed to be unedgicatable, and therefore are just moved through the system."

January 9, 2004 Referring to Catholic schools' willingness to educate children with learning disabilities. Sounding a bit unedgicatable at the White House.

PRESIDENTIAL SPEAK

"Old Doc Hastings has made a pretty good hand. He informed me first thing, before he even said hello, that he was a grandfather again—today. So, congratulations, Doc. I wouldn't take too much credit for it, Doc, if I were you."

August 22, 2003 *Setting United States Congressman Doc Hastings straight.* Speaking in Burbank, Washington.

"…We'll move together to ensure that the Iraqi people now got the capacity to run their own country. It's gonna take a time to get there."

February 2, 2004 Impressing our European allies during a press conference with French President Chirac at the G8 Summit in Evian, France.

The Very Curious Language of George W. Bush™
Volume 3

PRESIDENTIALSPEAK

"She's doing a fine job of coordinating interagency. She's doing what her—I mean—it shouldn'a—the, the, the role of the national security advisor is to not only provide good advice to the President, which she does on a regular basis—I value her judgment and her intelligence—uhh—but, uhh—her job is also to deal interagency, and to help unstick things that may get stuck—is the best way to put it. She's an unsticker."

October 28, 2003 *Referring to Condoleezza Rice, the national security 'unsticker'. White House, Washington, D.C.*

★ ★ ★ ★

"And Ralph Waycott, he is the volunteer coordinator for the Rancho Sierra Vista Nursery. I don't know if Ralph was a botanist in college or not, but it sure sounded like it."

August 15, 2003 *I remember the time I was an economist in college... before I changed my major — Editor.* Speaking at the Santa Monica Mountains National Recreation Area in California.

"I fully understand this is going to be a difficult process. I fully understand we need to work with our friends such as France to achieve the process."

February 2, 2003 Referring to attempts at achieving a peaceful solution to strife in the Middle East. And yes, hoping to achieve the process at the G8 Summit in Evian, France.

PRESIDENTIAL SPEAK

"I want to thank all of y'all for workin' so hard to help citizens make the right choice… to help people understand the need for healthier lives in America."

February 2, 2004 Speaking at the White House during a ceremony kicking off American Heart Month.

"I want to thank all the survivors of heart disease who are here. I asked the vice president what he was up to. He said he was headin' to the treadmill."

February 2, 2004 Proclaiming February as American Heart Month at a White House ceremony.

PRESIDENTIAL SPEAK

"There is no doubt in my mind that this country cannot achieve any objective we put our mind to."

Aoril 20, 2004 Speaking in New York.

"There is a lot of investigations going on about the intelligence service."

February 8, 2004 *There am?* Referring to faulty intelligence concerning Iraq's weapons of mass destruction. Speaking with Tim Russert on NBC's Meet the Press.

"The world is more peaceful and more free under my leadership."

October 28, 2003 *The President of the World — I mean United States — speaking from his office in the White House. Washington, D.C.*

PRESIDENTIAL SPEAK

"David McDounough, the principal of the school, said this: 'We bombard them'—that would be his students—'we bombard them with love.'"

January 9, 2004 Referring to a catholic school principal at a ceremony in the White House for the Catholic Education Association.

"I appreciate General Conway. This isn't the first time I met him. He looks you right in the eye. He's the kind of commander I'd like to serve under—just that he serves under me."

August 14, 2003 Referring to Lt. Gen. James Conway, commanding officer, One Marine Expeditionary Force. Marine Corps Air Station, Miramar, California.

The Very Curious Language of George W. Bush™
Volume 3

"There's a lot of responsibilities that come with running a company."

January 30, 2003 *There's a lot of responsibilities that come with running a country, too.* Speaking at the Boys' and Girls' Club of Greater Washington, D.C.

★ ★ ★ ★

"I had the opportunity to go out to Goree Island and talk about what slavery meant to America. It's very interesting when you think about it. The slaves who left here to go to America, because of their steadfast and their religion and their belief in freedom, helped change America."

July 8, 2003 *It is interesting but my own steadfast is wearing out.* Dakar, Senegal.

★ ★ ★ ★

"I recently met with the finance minister of the Palestinian Authority—was very impressed by his grasp of finances."

May 29, 2003 Speaking in Washington, D.C.

"America stands for liberty, for the pursuit of happiness and for the unalieinalienable right of life."

November 5, 2003 *Not easy for anyone to pronounce.* Washington, D.C.

"I think it's interesting. I'm a follower of American politics."

August 8, 2003 *What a stunning revelation.* Response when asked about Arnold Schwarzenegger running for governor of California. Crawford, Texas.

PRESIDENTIAL SPEAK

Reporter: "I wonder if either of these two pilots could describe their experience?"

Bush: "Yeah, sure they can. That's up to them. They don't have to, but—I have to speak to the press, they don't have to, but it's not that bad an experience."

April 20, 2003 Meeting with former POWs at Fort Hood, Texas.

★ ★ ★ ★

"Some of the other members of the crew are here as well. Where are they Robbie? Where are the members of your crew? Well, they musta couldn't pass the security check."

December 2, 2003 Speaking to Robbie Reiser, crew chief to NASCAR driver Matt Kenseth at White House ceremony.

PRESIDENTIAL SPEAK

"I call upon all nations to do everything they can to stop these terrorist killers. Thank you. Now watch this drive."

August 4, 2002 Speaking to the press during a round of golf. Kennebunkport, Maine.

"The Iraqi regime is a great threat to the United States. The Iraqi regime is a threat to any American and to threats who are friends of America."

January 3, 2003 *Making very clear the great threat posed by Iraq.* Speaking to troops at Fort Hood, Texas.

"We have a forward strategy of freedom in the Middle East."

February 8, 2004 *Must keep the strategy on a forward orientation.* Appearing on NBC's Meet the Press with Tim Russert.

The Very Curious Language of George W. Bush™
Volume 3

PRESIDENTIAL SPEAK

"I think I've answered the question, and yes, [Arnold Schwarzenegger] would be a good governor, as would others running for governor of California. Like you, I'm most interested in seeing how the process evolves. It's a fascinating bit of political drama evolving in the state—in the country's largest state."

August 13, 2003 'Largest state'... well, except for Alaska and Texas. Speaking from the nation's second largest state, Texas.

"Oftentimes, we live in a processed world—you know, people focus on the process and not results."

May 29, 2003 Speaking in Washington, D.C.

"It [the Stanley Cup] showed up at the Bob Edmunds restaurant in Brunswick, Ohio. Went to Filthy McNasty's Bar and Grill in Toronto. I don't know who took it there but I'll bet you're pretty happy the cup can't talk—if you know what I mean."

September 29, 2003 Welcoming the Stanley Cup champion New Jersey Devils to the White House.

"When an Arkansas tells a typical story—she talks about the fact that her husband was laid off from his job at a local steel mill."

January 7, 2003 A Texas speaking at the Economic Club in Chicago.

PRESIDENTIAL SPEAK

"They tell me this cup is 110 years old. That makes it older than the Oval Office. Umm, I see it's got all the names of the players who've won it, and now your names are on it. It's a fantastic legacy to athleticism and desire and drive. Umm, a couple of cuts here and there. Maybe a missed tooth or two."

September 29, 2003 Welcoming the Stanley Cup champion New Jersey Devils to the White House.

"I don't bring God into my life to—to, you know, kind of be a political person."

April 24, 2003 Interview with Tom Brokaw of NBC News.

"Well, you know, they were—first of all, they were the encouraging people. They were the ones who offered encouragement. I was, believe this or not, somewhat taken aback when I was in their presence. And these guys were so uplifting and so positive and so obviously thrilled to be here. They got in last night at midnight. They can speak for themselves. I think you can speak for yourselves. At least you did in my presence."

April 20, 2003 Please, speak for yourselves. Fort Hood, Texas.

★ ★ ★ ★

PRESIDENTIAL SPEAK

"I love the idea of a school in which people come to get educated and stay in the state in which they're educated."

August 13, 2002 Waco, Texas.

"I'm more worried about families finding job and putting food on the table than I am about economic theory and economic numbers."

August 13, 2003 *The usual tense confoundment while speaking to the press.* Crawford, Texas.

"I'm the master of low expectations."

June 4, 2003 Speaking to the press onboard Air Force One.

"See, it is a capital-intensive business. It requires sophisticated machinery to run this business, as the folks who work here know, it's purty darn sophisticated, idn't it?"

January 9, 2003 Speaking in Alexandria, Virginia, at the National Capital Flag Company.

★ ★ ★ ★

"Last year alone, it's important for our fellow citizens all across America to know that catastrophic wildflower—fires—burnt about 7 million acres of land."

August 11, 2004 Summerhaven, Arizona.

★ ★ ★ ★

"America has got some wonderful citizenry who just refuse to be defeated."

November 4, 2003 *It's correct, I suppose, but 'curious' nonetheless – Editor.* Harbison Canyon, California.

"I do think it would be helpful to get the United Nations in to help write a constitution. I mean, they're good at that."

September 22, 2003 *They're good at that and so many other things.* Interview aired on Fox Network.

"I'm not—not any intention of second-guessing his tactics. We share the same outcome."

July 9, 2003 Sharing outcomes in Pretoria, South Africa.

"A free society is one in which will mean more likely a peaceful partner in a troubled neighborhood."

May 5, 2003 *Troubled in more ways than one.* Little Rock, Arkansas.

★ ★ ★ ★

"Abolishing the double-taxation will increase the return on responsible investing, which will draw more money into the markets, which will make it easier for people to have capital to build plant and equipment."

January 9, 2003 Speaking at the National Capital Flag Company in Alexandria, Virginia.

★ ★ ★ ★

"And, listen, we're making good progress in Iraq. Sometimes it's hard to tell it when you listen to the filter."

October 6, 2003 *Please, please, please, don't be fooled by the "Filter" - the fourth estate, the independent press — the one thing, perhaps above all, that defines and is ultimately responsible for freedom in the United States of America. But, Mr. President, you know that. You're the President of this great country after all. — The Editor.* Washington, D.C.

★ ★ ★ ★

"At home, we'll protect our assets. We'll conserve our beautiful environment, and at the same time we'll work to make sure the people can make a living, the people can work hard—put money on the table."

August 22, 2003 *I prefer food on my table — Editor.* Speaking in Burbank, Washington.

★ ★ ★ ★

"This is historic times."

October 8, 2003 *They sure is.* Washington, D.C.

★ ★ ★ ★

"In 2001, we passed what's called the 'No Child Left Behind' legislation. I love that phrase because it's a commitment of our nation to make sure that not only does every child excel, but no child gets left behind. Members of both parties of Republicans and Democrats came together to pass this law."

April 30, 2003 Washington, D.C.

★ ★ ★ ★

PRESIDENTIAL SPEAK

"I also wanna thank Ben Nighthorse Campbell who's over from the great state of Colorado. Colorado has also faced a lotta fire, too many fire."

August 11, 2003 Referring to the U.S. Senator from Colorado. Speaking on forest management in Summerhaven, Arizona.

"You cannot lead America to a positive tomorrow with revenge on one's mind. Revenge is so incredibly negative."

March 23, 2000 Interview with The Washington Post.

"I mean, he's a man who has presided over suiciders…"

November 16, 2003 The ulcer medications continue to flow at the Webster Dictionary offices. Aired on BBC Breakfast with Frost.

The Very Curious Language of George W. Bush™
Volume 3

PRESIDENTIAL SPEAK

"The stock market started to decline in March of 2000. Uh, that was the first signs that things were troubled."

February 8, 2004 *Word-tense trailblazing for the umpteenth time.* Speaking on NBC's Meet The Press.

"We're fighting an enemy that knows no rules of law, that will wear civilian uniforms..."

March 25, 2003 *I'm wearing my civilian uniform right now. My wife likes a man in a uniform... and I do look quite dashing — Editor.* Speaking at the Pentagon. Arlington, Virginia.

"I've got a foreign policy that is, um, one that believes America has a responsibility in this world to lead."

February 8, 2004 *Personification of America's foreign policy.* Speaking in the Oval Office to Tim Russert on NBC's Meet the Press.

"Not everybody agrees with [forest] thinning. There'll be objections. But we want those objections heard, of course. Every citizen needs to hear a voice."

August 11, 2003 *I know I'm hearing voices – Editor.* Speaking on the topic of forest management. Summerhaven, Arizona.

"This administration is committed to your effort, and with the support of Congress we will continue to work to provide the resources school need to fund the era of reform."

January 8, 2003 Speaking at the White House, celebrating the anniversary of the No Child Left Behind Act.

PRESIDENTIAL SPEAK

"We had a good cabinet meeting. Talked about a lot of issues. Secretary of state and defense brought us up to date about our desires to spread freedom and peace around the world."

August 1, 2003 Remarking to the press after a White House cabinet meeting. Washington, D.C.

★ ★ ★ ★

"There's gonna be ample time for the American people to assess whether or not I made a good calls."

February 8, 2004 *For the love of… please, Mr. President, stop talking like this—so I can get on with my other work! – Editor.* Referring to his decision to invade Iraq. Speaking in the Oval Office to Tim Russert of NBC News.

★ ★ ★ ★

The Very Curious Language of George W. Bush™
Volume 3

PRESIDENTIAL SPEAK

"You see, the enemies want to create a sense of fear and intrepidation."

October 8, 2003 *I just love this one, such classic George W. Bush – Editor.* Speaking in Washington, D.C.

"I appreciate all the members of Congress here. I pray for your wisdom on a daily basis."

February 6, 2003 Speaking at the National Prayer Breakfast at the Washington Hilton in Washington, D.C.

"This nation of ours should not be fearful of faith. We oughta welcome faith to help solve many of the nation's seemingly intractilable problems."

August 24, 2003 *Not the only problem that's intractilable.* Speaking at a fundraiser in Portland, Oregon.

PRESIDENTIAL SPEAK

"Our actions in Iraq are part of a duty we have accepted across the world. We're keeping our resolves and we will stay focused on the war on terror."

August 14, 2003 Speaking at the Marine Corps Air Station in Miramar, California.

"I can assure you that, even though I won't be sitting through every single moment of the seminars, nor will the vice president, we will look at the summaries."

August 13, 2002 *Putting to rest any concern – what a relief.* Waco, Texas.

PRESIDENTIAL SPEAK

"Well, it is your park. It's the park of every person who lives in America. And we gotta remember that. We're stewards of the people land."

August 15, 2003 Speaking at the Santa Monica Mountains National Recreation Area in California.

"The world is a better place when we got rid of Saddam Hussein."

October 3, 2003 *As usual, taking great liberties with tense formation.* Milwaukee, Wisconsin.

"I'm honored to be with the men and women of NASA. I want to thank those of you who have come in person. I welcome those who are listening by video."

January 14, 2004 Announcing his new vision for U.S. space exploration. NASA Headquarters, Washington, D.C.

PRESIDENTIAL SPEAK

"And the threat of Saddam Hussein was a unique threat in this sense—the world recognized he was a threat for twelve years, and seventeen resolutions, I think it is. I believe it was seventeen resolutions. For the resolution counter, give me a hand here— seventeen? Seventeen resolutions. And he ignored them."

December 15, 2003 Speaking in Washington, D.C., with the assistance of the Resolution Counter.

"Our opportunity in society must also be a compassionate society."

July 28, 2003 Pittsburgh, Pennsylvania.

PRESIDENTIAL SPEAK

"Al-Qaida is a group of people that they don't care about taking innocent life."

May 13, 2003 *An extra word never hurt anything.*

★ ★ ★ ★

"You know, let me, let me talk about al-Qaida just for a second. I—I made the statement that we're dismantling senior management, and we are. Our people have done a really good job of hauling in a lot of the key operators: Khalid Sheik Mohammed, Abu Zubaydah, Ramzi, ahh—Ramzi al Shibh, or whatever the guy's name was."

July 30, 2003 White House, Washington, D.C.

★ ★ ★ ★

PRESIDENTIALSPEAK

"I appreciate Dwight Adams who's the director of the FBI laboratory. He just gave me a fine tour. It's a pretty sophisticated facilities."

September 9, 2003 Speaking at the FBI Academy in Quantico, Virginia.

★ ★ ★ ★

"There's no doubt in my mind that we should allow the world's worst leaders to hold America hostage, to threaten our peace, to threaten our friends and allies with the world's worst weapons."

September 5, 2002 Speaking at a fundraising dinner in South Bend, Indiana.

★ ★ ★ ★

PRESIDENTIAL SPEAK

Bush: "I don't know what you're talking about, about international law. I've got to consult my lawyer."

Reporter: "Can I clarify one thing?"

Bush: "Yes, you may clarify something."

Reporter: "Thank you very much."

Bush: "Depends on what it is, though."

December 11, 2003 Washington, D.C.

"I said you were a man of peace. I want you to know I took immense crap for that."

June 3, 2003 *No comment – Editor.* Conversation with Israeli Prime Minister Ariel Sharon, as reported in The Washington Post and elsewhere.

"Between those who work for peaceful change and those who adopt a methods of gangsters... there is no neutral ground."

September 23, 2003 Referring to terrorists. Speaking to the U.N. General Assembly.

"We got into deficit because the economy went into the recession— is how we got into deficit."

May 5, 2003 *Feeling more contented about having pursued my graduate work at Cornell rather than Harvard. – Editor.* Speaking in Little Rock, Arkansas.

"Work is not done. There's still dangers and challenges to remain."

April 24, 2003 *At my own expense, I'll fly in my 5th grade teacher for an Oval Office lesson and attempt to straighten out this problem once and for all – Editor.* Lima, Ohio.

PRESIDENTIAL SPEAK

"We'll get to the bottom of this and move on. But I want to tell you something—leaks of classified information are a bad thing, and we've had them. There's too much leaking in Washington. That's just the way it is. And we've had leaks out of the administrative branch, had leaks out of the legislative branch, and out of the executive branch and the legislative branch, and I've spoken out consistently against them and I want to know who the leakers are."

September 30, 2003 *Well if we can't find the leakers in the Executive Branch, look carefully at those no good *@+#^*&%@ in the administrative branch. They never could be trusted. Speaking in Chicago, Illinois. (Note to our international readers: There is no Administrative Branch of the U.S. Government.)*

PRESIDENTIAL SPEAK

"Coalition forces have encountered serious violence in some areas of Iraq. Our military commanders report that this violence is being intickated by three groups."

April 13, 2004 White House press conference. Washington, D.C.

"I appreciate my friend Tom Ridge. See, we were both governors at one time. So I got to know him as a governor of a relatively small state—Pennsylvania."

September 10, 2003 Referring to Secretary of Homeland Security Tom Ridge. Speaking in Quantico, Virginia, at the FBI Academy.

The Very Curious Language of George W. Bush™
Volume 3

"I also thank the first responders from the nearby communities who are with us today. You're the ones America's count on in times of emergency."

September 10, 2003 Speaking at the FBI Academy in Quantico, Virginia.

"I need to be able to move the right people to the right place at the right time to protect you, and I'm not going to accept a lousy bill out of the United Nations Senate."

October 31, 2002 Tangled up in South Bend, Indiana.

PRESIDENTIAL SPEAK

"For the sake of job growth, let's put those tax cuts we've already got in place, in place today so people can find work."

May 2, 2003 *Ah, yes, tax cuts. The cure-all for everything that ails us.* Santa Clara, California.

"I appreciate very much Larry Penley. He's been the coach. He's been there for only two decades. It's taken awhile to get it right."

November 17, 2003 Congratulating (sort of) Clemson University Men's Golf Coach Larry Penley for his team's NCAA championship season.

"We want to make sure our wallets all across the country are healthy."

January 31, 2004 *Here's to healthy wallets.* Philadelphia, Pennsylvania.

"Now, there are governors around the state and the country that—that have said, look, give us the flexibility to be able to dovetail the Head Start program into our preschool programs so that all students—so we have a better control over whether or not the students are given the skills necessary so that when hold us to account we can achieve that which we want to achieve, which is excellence in the classroom."

July 7, 2003 *Excellently put.* Landover, Maryland.

PRESIDENTIALSPEAK

"… And I'm real proud that you're here. So I asked 'em once again, 'are you going to be back next year?' They said, 'How 'bout you?'"

November 17, 2003 Welcoming the returning NCAA national champion Princeton University women's lacrosse team to the White House.

★ ★ ★ ★

"Our productivity is high. I hope some of it has to do—I know some of it has to do, I hope you understand some of it has to do with the fact that the role of government can help create growth."

December 5, 2003 Clarification in Halethorpe, Maryland.

★ ★ ★ ★

PRESIDENTIAL SPEAK

"I expressed our nation's condolences at the needless murder of innocent people by the latest suicider."

October 6, 2003 Washington, D.C.

★ ★ ★ ★

"There is such hope here in Northern Ireland that the past can be broken."

April 8, 2003 *I'd like to see that – Editor.* Belfast, Northern Ireland.

★ ★ ★ ★

"We're encouraged to see more Iraqs take responsibility for resolving the standoff in Najaf."

October 6, 2003 *Go your Iraqs.* Washington, D.C.

★ ★ ★ ★

PRESIDENTIAL SPEAK

"Bernice Welchel is the principal of, uh, City Springs Elementary School right here in Baltimore, Maryland…uh, close here to Baltimore, Maryland."

January 8, 2003 Speaking at the White House in Washington, D.C., about the No Child Left Behind Act.

"See, we want everybody in this country—every person, we want the addict, we want the single lonely mom, we want the child, the dyslexic child—all to feel a part of the future of this country."

October 29, 2003 Dallas, Texas.

The Very Curious Language of George W. Bush™
Volume 3

PRESIDENTIAL SPEAK

"I show up when they need me to call people to account, to praise, or to say, wait a minute. You told me in Jordan that you would do this. You haven't done it. Why? How come? What is it? It's to keep the thing moving, keep the processes moving. They've got the man on the ground that is going to—he's just going to—I used the expression, 'ride herd'. I don't know if anybody understood the meaning. It's a little informal in diplomatic terms. I said, 'We're going to put a guy on the ground to ride herd on the process.' See them all scratching their heads."

June 4, 2003 *Feeling self-congratulatory over having stumped a group of multi-lingual statesmen with a regional American colloquialism. Talking about his meeting with Palestinian and Israeli leaders onboard Air Force One.*

PRESIDENTIAL SPEAK

"They're good, strong men. It's an amazing experience, when you think about it. Here we are, Easter, the great—one of the great religious holidays, and these guys arrived last night. Might have actually arrived Easter day. I don't know if it was exactly midnight, or a little after midnight."

April 20, 2003 *Pinning down the time.* Fort Hood, Texas.

"In order for this road map, which is a way to get to a peaceful settlement, people have got to assume responsibility."

October 6, 2003 *Granted, the point is made, but...* Washington, D.C.

The Very Curious Language of George W. Bush™
Volume 3

"We ended the rule of one of history's worst tyrants, and in so doing we not only freed the American people, we made our own people more secure."

May 3, 2003 *Thank goodness. For a minute there I thought I wasn't free – Editor.* Speaking to the press in Crawford, Texas, during a visit by Australian Prime Minister John Howard.

Bush: "I was hoping to run into a fellow Texan today. His excellency, Gregory Amon, is the bishop from Austin, Texas."
Voice from audience: "Yeeehaa!"
Bush: "I'm glad there's only a handful of Texans here."

January 9, 2004 Speaking in the White House to the Catholic Educational Association.

PRESIDENTIAL SPEAK

"And one of the greatest societal needs is we have is to make sure our guys that spent time in the pen, not only receives spiritual guidance and love, but spiritual guidance and love can only go so far."

July 16, 2003 *Providing a very exacting summation with respect to those 'guys in the pen'. Washington, D.C.*

"I'd rather have them sacrificing on behalf of our nation than, you know, endless hours of testimony on Congressional Hill."

June 4, 2002 *Referring to U.S. intelligence agency personnel. Speaking to the press at the National Security Agency's operations center, Fort Meade, Maryland. (For our international readers: it's 'Capitol Hill'.)*

PRESIDENTIALSPEAK

Reporter: "How would you describe the personal relationship between Chancellor Schroeder and yourself?"

Bush: "Uh, the, uh, the Chancellor has got a good sense of humor and uh, therefore he is able to, uh, uh, make me laugh and a person that can make me laugh is a person who is easy to be with and a person who is easy to be with means I've got a comfortable relationship with him."

February 27, 2004 During a visit to the White House by German Chancellor Gerhardt Schroeder.

★ ★ ★ ★

PRESIDENTIAL SPEAK

"And then we'll be going to Goree Island, where I'll be giving a speech about race—race in the world, race as it relates to Africa and America. And we're in the process of writing it. I can't give you any highlights of the speech yet because I, frankly, haven't seen it."

July 3, 2003 Waiting for the speech in Washington, D.C.

★ ★ ★ ★

"The students at Yale came from all different backgrounds and all parts of the country. Within months, I knew many of them."

Published November 1999 From *A Charge to Keep,* by George W. Bush

★ ★ ★ ★

PRESIDENTIAL SPEAK

"Whatever amount of energy and effort is required from the White House, we will provide it, to get a bill done this summer; one that I can sign and then we can all go back to our districts—in my case, tour the country."

June 25, 2003 Just prior to touring the country. Washington, D.C.

★ ★ ★ ★

"We had a great visit on the plane. There is no air raids on Air Force One, by the way."

October 3, 2003 Even my children, at times, become acutely embarrassed for their President. Milwaukee, Wisconsin.

★ ★ ★ ★

The Very Curious Language of George W. Bush™
Volume 3

"The second pillar of peace and security in our world is the willingness of free nations, when the last resort arrives, to retain aggression and evil by force."

November 19, 2003 *Lending enormous credence to the old maxim that America and England are 'divided by a common language'... and in doing so, making all of us Americans proud. London, England.*

★ ★ ★ ★

"By allowing businesses to expense up to $75,000 it means that somebody is more likely to buy a copy machine or, uh, in this case, an architectural-fancy machine."

January 22, 2003 *Speaking at J.S. Logistics in St. Louis, Missouri, purchasers of architectural-fancy machines and other fancy things.*

★ ★ ★ ★

PRESIDENTIAL SPEAK

Reporter: "Does the U.S. actually see Australia as its deputy sheriff in Southeast Asia?"

Bush: "No, we don't see it as a deputy sheriff; we see it as a sheriff. There's a difference."

October 19, 2003 You're under arrest. Bangkok, Thailand.

"The country needs our presence and will have our presence...needs our presence to help make sure that those remenates of al-Qaida that still lurk around the area will be brought to justice and they will be, they will be."

January 29, 2003 *Those remenates are still lurking, I fear.* Speaking at Devos Performance Hall in Grand Rapids, Michigan.

PRESIDENTIALSPEAK

"Any time we've got any kind of inkling that somebody is thinking about doing something to an American and something to our homeland, you've just got to know we're moving on it, to protect the United Nations Constitution, and at the same time, we're protecting you."

October 31, 2002 *Cross pollinating in Aberdeen, South Dakota.*

★ ★ ★ ★

"There's a lot of Pakistani Americans who are pleased you are here today, sir."

October 1, 2003 *One doesn't even notice after awhile – Editor. Washington, D.C.*

★ ★ ★ ★

PRESIDENTIALSPEAK

"One of the things that's interesting about the Stanley Cup is that the players—each player gets to spend time with it. Must be pretty neat. The cup has traveled throughout North America and Europe. It's been to some famous sites. Ah, recently it was at the McDonalds drive-thru in New Glasgow, Nova Scotia. Must have been a pretty interesting moment for that burger flipper—filler-up."

September 29, 2003 Welcoming the Stanley Cup champion New Jersey Devils to the White House.

★ ★ ★ ★

"The American people is this country's greatest asset."

February 12, 2003 Alexandria, Virginia.

The Very Curious Language of George W. Bush™
Volume 3

PRESIDENTIAL SPEAK

"There's a reason why the world asked Saddam Hussein to disarm—for twelve years. And the reason why is because he's dangerous, he's used 'em. He's tortures his own people. He's gassed his own people. He's attacked people in the neighborhood."

January 29, 2003 *And he's got what was coming to him.* Speaking at Devos Performance Hall in Grand Rapids, Michigan.

★ ★ ★ ★

"And, obviously, the more help we can get, the more we appreciate it. And we are continuing to work with other nations to ask their help advice."

July 21, 2003 Needing help advice in Crawford, Texas.

PRESIDENTIAL SPEAK

"You know, the world looks at us and say, 'They're strong,' and we are. We're strong militarily. We've got a greater strength than that. We've got a, a strength in the universonality of human rights and the human condition."

January 31, 2003 *At this point the world looks at us and say lots of other things besides 'They're strong.' Can't argue with the universonality thing though — Editor.* Speaking at the Dwight D. Eisenhower Executive Office Building in Washington, D.C.

"In 2000 alone, obesity costs totaled the country an estimated cost of $117 billion."

July 18, 2003 Speaking in Dallas, Texas.

PRESIDENTIAL SPEAK

"The ambassador and the general were briefing me on the—the vast majority of Iraqis want to live in a peaceful, free world. And we will find these people and we will bring them to justice."

October 27, 2003 *Bring 'em all to justice. They've got some nerve. As always, dispensing clear, articulate policy from the White House, Washington, D.C.*

★ ★ ★ ★

"And the men up here represent a representative sample of what we call the faith community in America. People who first and foremost have been called because of a calling much higher than government."

July 16, 2003 *I'm beginning to resent the representation represented by the calling for which I've been called — Editor in distress. Washington, D.C.*

The Very Curious Language of George W. Bush™
Volume 3

PRESIDENTIAL SPEAK

"I was disappointed that the Congress did not respond to the $3.5 billion we asked for. They not only reduced the budget that we asked for, they earmarked a lot of the money. That's a disappointment, a disappointment when the executive branch gets micromanaged by the legislative branch."

February 24, 2003 *BAD legislative branch!* Washington, D.C.

"No, I know all the war rhetoric, but it's all aimed at achieving peace."

August 7, 2002 *Well, it didn't work.* Madison Central High School, Madison, Mississippi.

The Very Curious Language of George W. Bush™
Volume 3

PRESIDENTIAL SPEAK

"Our country puts $1 billion a year up to help feed the hungry, and we're by far the most generous nation in the world when it comes to that, and I'm proud to report that. This isn't a contest of who's the most generous. I'm just telling you as an aside. We're generous. We shouldn't be bragging about it, but we are. We're very generous."

July 16, 2003 *Trying not to brag... and failing. Washington, D.C.*

"My views are one that speaks to freedom."

February 18, 2004 *Plural, singular, plural, singular, plural, singular, plural, singular, plural, singular,.................. Washington, D.C.*

PRESIDENTIAL SPEAK

"I came to seize opportunities, and not let them slip away. We are meeting the tests of our time. Terrorists declared war on the United States and war is what they got."

June 17, 2003 *Summing up the "opportunity" to engage in war. Washington, D.C.*

"The American people know that Saddam Hussein has weapons of mass destruction. By the way, he declared he didn't have any."

March 6, 2003 *Speaking at the White House on behalf of the American people.*

PRESIDENTIAL SPEAK

"Leaders in the region speak of a new Arab charter that champions internal reform, greater politics participation, economic openness, and free trade. And from Morocco to Bahrain and beyond, nations are taking genuine steps towards politics reform."

February 26, 2003 Washington, D.C.

★ ★ ★ ★

"I particularly want to thank the four folks who have recovered from homelessness and addiction to alcohol and drugs."

February 10, 2003 Speaking in Nashville, Tennessee, about the 'recovering' homeless population.

★ ★ ★ ★

"I remember a 'baby doc' that came to see me when I was in Pennsylvania. She had tears in hers eyes. She said, 'I love to deliver babies. I can't do it anymore.'"

January 29, 2003 *Her is a sad story.* Speaking at Devos Performance Hall in Grand Rapids, Michigan.

★ ★ ★ ★

"That's the basic principles of the faith-based initiative which you've heard a lot about."

July 16, 2003 *Please children, speak as I should, not as I do.* Washington, D.C.

★ ★ ★ ★

"Israel must make sure there's a continuous territory that the Palestinians can call home."

June 3, 2003 *With the benefit of the official White House transcript, we come to learn that 'contiguous' was the intended word.* Sharm el-Sheikh, Egypt.

PRESIDENTIAL SPEAK

"It used to be, you know, when you talked about stocks and bonds, it probably wasn't all that long ago you'd say, 'Well gosh, how's your portfolio?' and that would probably pertain to, you know, a handful of people that lived, you know, I dunno, uh, knew something about Wall Street."

February 12, 2003 Speaking at Charles Schwab & Company in Alexandria, Virginia.

"Listen, I recognize there's going to be extremes, particularly in the Palestinian territories, that want to blow up peace."

June 9, 2003 *Damn those extremes.* Washington, D.C.

The Very Curious Language of George W. Bush™
Volume 3

PRESIDENTIAL SPEAK

"The [military] academies are really important for a lot of reasons. Obviously, what you learn on the football field is even more important since we're still at war."

May 16, 2003 Presenting the Commander-In-Chief's Trophy to the Air Force Academy football team. The White House, Washington, D.C.

"There are some who feel like that the conditions [in Iraq] are such that they can attack us there. My answer is: Bring 'em on!"

July 2, 2003 On behalf of all the family members of U.S. Armed Forces personnel serving in Iraq – "Thanks a lot." Speaking in Washington, D.C.

PRESIDENTIAL SPEAK

"I think we're making progress. We understand where the power of this country lay. It lays in the hearts and souls of Americans. It must lay in our pocketbooks. It lays in the willingness for people to work hard. But as importantly, it lays in the fact that we've got citizens from all walks of life, all political parties, that are willing to say: 'I want to love my neighbor.'"

April 11, 2001 Lying down the rules of grammar in Concord, North Carolina.

★ ★ ★ ★

"I always, always—sometimes—say, government can hand out money…"

March 3, 2004 Los Angeles, California.

"Uh, the economic stimulus plan that I passed,—or, I passed, I asked Congress to pass, I worked with Congress to pass—is making a big difference."

February 8, 2004 *It's late and I'm tired… it's enough that it passed — a weary Editor.* Speaking with Tim Russert on NBC's *Meet the Press.*

"These despicable [suicide attacks] were committed by killers whose only faith is hate. And the United States will find the killers, and they will learn the meaning of American justice."

May 13, 2003 *Strictly speaking, the killers are permanently unavailable to be taught the lessons of American justice.* Denouncing suicide bombings in Saudi Arabia. Speaking in Indianapolis, Indiana.

"Laura reminded me - in July of 2002, on the television screens, came to the notation: 'America is Marching to War.'"

February 26, 2004 Speaking in Louisville, Kentucky.

"We've got people workin' hard in intelligence-gathering around the world to get as good an information as possible."

February 8, 2004 *Let's hope it's as good an information as possible.* Discussing the "War on Terror" with Tim Russert of NBC's *Meet the Press.*

"We've got to make sure there is more affordable homes."

July 16, 2003 *Children, cover your ears.* Washington, D.C.

PRESIDENTIALSPEAK

"Danny Ferry is here? Where is Danny Ferry? Yes, there he is. He and I share an interesting relationship. As you may know, his father, Bob, won the NBA championship ring. And so Danny and Bob Ferry are only the second father-son combination to ever win a championship ring, if you get my drift. We're members of the 'famous fathers club.' And, anyway, I want to welcome you here. You'll see where the—only the second son of a President offices is in a minute."

October 14, 2003 *I get your drift, but only your drift.* A mere minute away from the Oval Office. Washington, D.C.

★ ★ ★ ★

PRESIDENTIAL SPEAK

"If those killers, those criminals, believe that their bloody criminal acts will shake even one hair off the body of our nation and its unity, then they are deceiving themselves."

May 13, 2003 Referring to suicide bombings in Riyadh, Saudi Arabia. Indianapolis, Indiana.

"There's serious consequences if you don't [disarm]—and that was a unanimous verdict. In other words, the world, through the U.N. Security Council, said that we're unanimous, and you're danger."

February 8, 2004 *Danger, danger everywhere.* Referring to Iraq during an interview with Tim Russert of NBC News.

"I need some ribs... I'm hungry and I'm going to order some ribs... I'm ordering ribs... do you need a rib?... Ribs? Good. Let's order up some ribs."

January 22, 2004 *Moving in a very straight line toward the target.* Remarks to the Press Pool. Nothin' Fancy Café, Rosewell, New Mexico.

"I've got a vision for what I wanna do for the country. See, I know exactly where I wanna lead. I wanna lead us to—I wanna lead this world to a more peace and freedom."

February 8, 2004 *I've been looking for a more peace and freedom my whole life... and finally, someone to lead me there – Editor.* Speaking on NBC's *Meet the Press* with host, Tim Russert.

PRESIDENTIAL SPEAK

Tim Russert: "Biggest issues in the upcoming campaign?"

Bush: "…and who understands that the true strength of this country, uh, uh, is the hearts and souls of the American citizens."

February 8, 2004 *Demonstrating splendorous tense alignment, per usual.* Speaking from the Oval Office on NBC's *Meet the Press.*

"I glance at the headlines just to kind of get a flavor for what's moving. I rarely read the stories, and get briefed by people who… probably read the news themselves."

September 21, 2003 *Dear Lord, let's hope so.* Interview with Brit Hume on Fox News Channel. Washington, D.C.

The Very Curious Language of George W. Bush™
Volume 3

"You see, when Al and his company decides to buy a machine, somebody has got to make the machine. And that means somebody in the machine-making company is more likely to find a job, as well."

October 3, 2003 *Unless they already have one.* Speaking in Milwaukee, Wisconsin.

★ ★ ★ ★

"Dr. [Raja] Khuzai also was there to have Thanksgiving dinner with our troops. And it turned out to be me, as well."

March 12, 2004 Dr. Khuzai is a member of the Iraqi Governing Council. The President is referring to his own surprise visit to Baghdad on Thanksgiving Day, 2003. Washington, D.C.

★ ★ ★ ★

"The country was resilient, tough and strong—determined to defeat terror and determined to go about our life no matter what the threat."

February 12, 2003 Speaking at Charles Schwab & Company in Alexandria, Virginia, while the country goes about our lives.

★ ★ ★ ★

"Right here in the Oval Office I sat down with, uh, Mr. Pachechi and Chalabi and Al Hakim, uh—people from different parts of the country—that have made the firm commitment that they want a, uh, constitutional eventually written…"

February 8, 2004 *Looking forward to the development of Iraq's Constitutional.* Speaking with Tim Russert while taping NBC's *Meet the Press* in the Oval Office.

★ ★ ★ ★

PRESIDENTIALSPEAK

"I know there's a lot of young ladies who are growing up wondering whether or not they can be champs. And they see the championship teams from USC and University of Portland here—girls who worked hard to get to where they are, and they're wondering about the example they're setting. What is life choices about?"

February 24, 2003 *The ongoing torture of the nation's English teachers shows no sign of abating.* White House. (USC = University of Southern California...for our international readers.)

★ ★ ★ ★

"In 1994, there were 67 schools in Texas that were rated 'exemplorary' according to our own tests."

October 5, 1999 *The linguistic damage always seems worse when the topic is education.* Manhattan Institute for Policy Research, New York.

"There's a lot of things that there's misconceptions. Evidently it's a misconceptions that Americans believe that Muslims are terrorists."

October 22, 2003 Speaking onboard Air Force One, mercifully out of range of most of the listening world.

★ ★ ★ ★

"The House of Representatives will take up this issue in the coming weeks, under the leadership of a man from Illinois, a guy who I've got a lot of respect from—Speaker Denny Hastert."

June 11, 2003 Chicago, Illinois.

★ ★ ★ ★

"It's a commission not only to convince our fellow citizens to love one another just like we like to be loved. It's a commission also to devise practical ways to encourage others to serve. And one practical way is for the development of an award that Americans from all walks of life all around our country will be able to post boldly on their wall, that says. 'I served this great country by loving somebody.'"

January 30, 2003 *This is a great country and now I want my award. I earned it. I deserve it. And I most assuredly will post it boldly on my wall. Mailing address is Outland Books, P.O. Box 534, Skaneateles, NY 13152. Washington, D.C.*

"We can outcompete with anybody."

March 11, 2004 *One way or another, Mr. President. Bay Shore, New York.*

PRESIDENTIAL SPEAK

"The basic tenets of Islam is peace and respect and tolerance. And that's what they wanted to make the point to me, that we are—that's the way we are."

October 22, 2003 *It just sometimes doesn't seem believable that the most powerful human being on earth really does communicate in such a jumbled way — Editor.* Onboard Air Force One.

"I love the story of America. I love the fact that people who started with nothing and have built a fantastic food processing business."

October 14, 2003 Speaking in Fresno, California.

PRESIDENTIAL SPEAK

"More Muslims have died at the hands of killers than—I say more Muslims—a lot of Muslims have died—I don't know the exact count—at Istanbul. Look at these different places around the world where there's been tremendous death and destruction because killers kill."

February 18, 2004 *Killers do kill, there is solid evidence of that.* Washington, D.C.

★ ★ ★ ★

"I'm a war president. I make decisions here in the Oval Office in foreign policy matters with war on my mind."

February 8, 2004 *Oh, really — one wouldn't have noticed.* Speaking on NBC's Meet the Press.

PRESIDENTIAL SPEAK

"It's not a dictatorship in Washington, but I tried to make it one in that instance."

January 15, 2004 Referring to the executive order making federal funding available to faith-based organizations. Speaking in New Orleans, Louisiana.

"Congress wouldn't act, so I signed an executive order. That means I did it on my own."

March 3, 2004 *Congratulations.* Los Angeles, California.

"…nucular…nucular…nucular… nucular…nucular…nucular… nucular…nucular…nucular… nucular…nucular…"

May 23, 2003 *Demonstrating continued and unyielding intransigence over the pronounciation of this word.* Crawford, Texas.

PRESIDENTIAL SPEAK

"A president must set great goals, worthy of a great nation. We're a great nation, therefore a president must set big goals. I set a goal for this country to make the world more peaceful by spreading freedom. Freedom is not America's gift to the world; freedom is God's gift to each and every individual in the world. I set a great goal here at home."

October 29, 2003 *Freedom, or else! Dallas, Texas.*

★ ★ ★ ★

"There is all kinds of estimates about the cost of war... There's strong signals that this economy will improve."

February 25 and 27, 2003 *And again, and again, and... Washington, D.C.*

PRESIDENTIAL SPEAK

"We said loud and clear, if you cheat the shareholder and your employees, you will be held responsible for those decisions. The world is now more peaceful because we acted."

June 19, 2003 *Peace dividends all over the place.* Referring to corporate evildoers in Fridley, Minnesota.

"...The mighty Illini tennis team...the mighty Clemson golf team...the mighty Virginia Cavalier lacrosse team...the mighty Rice Owls..."

November 17, 2003 Demonstrating descriptive flair while introducing collegiate sports teams at a White House ceremony honoring the 2003 NCAA spring season national champions.

PRESIDENTIAL SPEAK

"But one of the problems of being a productive economy is that a worker can—one worker puts out. There's better output per worker, let me put it to you that way."

May 5, 2003 *Mesmerizing the uneducated among us with the heavyweight intellect honed at Yale University and Harvard Business School.* Little Rock, Arkansas.

★ ★ ★ ★

"The manufacturing sector has been hit. The textile industry has been hit. People have lost work. And yet in other sectors of the economy here in North Carolina are growing."

November 7, 2003 *Just one too many words, otherwise, perfect.* Winston-Salem, North Carolina.

★ ★ ★ ★

PRESIDENTIAL SPEAK

"Many doctors serve their fellow humans in the most compassionate ways. I went down to Mississippi, met a man who had moved to Mississippi to provide health care for some of our most neediest citizens."

March 4, 2003 *From one human to another, are you enjoying the latest (Mis)Speak? – Editor.* Speaking at the American Medical Association's national conference in Washington, D.C.

"It's hard to be successful if you don't make something somebody doesn't want to buy."

March 9, 2004 *How many times did you read this?* Arlington, Virginia.

PRESIDENTIAL SPEAK

"There was a poll that showed me going up yesterday—not to be on the defensive. Actually, I'm in pretty good shape politically, I really am. I didn't mean to sound defensive, but I am. Politicians, by the way, who pay attention to the polls are doomed—trying to chase opinion when what you need to do is lead, set the tone."

October 14, 2003 Doomed in Washington, D.C.

★ ★ ★ ★

"I think 2004 is going to be a great year. And in the spirit of great years, I'll answer a few questions."

January 1, 2004 *In the spirit of great years, I'll make a few editorial comments – Editor, of course.* Falfurrias, Texas.

PRESIDENTIAL SPEAK

"But there is a difference of opinion about who best to spend your money in Washington, D.C. Sometimes they forget whose money you're spending. Listen to the rhetoric."

January 22, 2003 *Whose money are you spending? Yeah, you.* St. Louis, Missouri.

"It's clear this guy [Saddam Hussein] could even care less about the first [U.N.] resolution... could care less about human condition inside Iraq."

February 18 & 25, 2003 *Petty I know, but it's 'couldn't care less', right?... I'll be getting letters over this one — Editor.* Washington, D.C.

The Very Curious Language of George W. Bush™
Volume 3

PRESIDENTIALSPEAK

"The March to War affected the people's confidence. It's hard to make investment. See, if you're a small business owner or a large business owner and you're thinking about investing, you've got to be optimistic when you invest. Except when you're marching to war, it's not a very optimistic thought, is it? In other words, it's the opposite of optimistic when you're thinking you're going to war."

February 9, 2004 *Is anyone else feeling opposite of optimistic? Springfield, Missouri.*

★ ★ ★ ★

"Small business owners like Joe may have problems passing their business off to a child or somebody they choose to pass their business off of."

January 22, 2003 Speaking in St. Louis, Missouri.

★ ★ ★ ★

"God loves you, and I love you. And you can count on both of us as a powerful message that people who wonder about their future can hear."

March 3, 2004 *I wonder quite considerably about my future and look forward to the powerful message — Editor.* Los Angeles, California.

★ ★ ★ ★

"I appreciate the desire for flexibility. I support the governor's desire for flexibility so long as, one: federal monies going to the states are used only for Head Start. In other words, what we really don't want to do is say we're going to focus on Head Start, the Head Start money goes for, you know, the prison complex. I know that won't happen with Governor Ehrlich but there needs to be a guarantee that the federal money spent on Head Start only go to Head Start. Secondly, states and local governments must put money into the program, which would lock in the Head Start money for Head Start. So, the flexibility given to the state would not allow the state's budget flexibility. Governors ought to have that flexibility to hope that Congress will provide that flexibility so that when the accountability systems kick in, fully kick in, that a governor can truthfully say, well, I've had the tools necessary to make sure the Head Start program fits into an overall comprehensive plan for literacy and math for every child in the state of Maryland—in Governor Ehrlich's case."

July 7, 2003 *Understood?* Speaking in Landover, Maryland.

"I think I'll leave the talent to my great friend, Michael W. Smith, and Sarah Paul Brummett. It's good to see Michael 'W'. I like a man whose middle name is 'W'."

February 10, 2003 Speaking at the Opryland Hotel in Nashville, Tennessee.

"Mark McLellan's here with us of the director of the Food and Drug Administration. I appreciate your leadership, Mark, on this, this incredibly important agency."

February 3, 2003 *On, of - of, on, what's the difference?* Speaking at the National Institutes of Health in Bethesda, Maryland.

"This country is a fabulous country because we've got good, honorable people who are willing to serve at all levels of government. And one of the key levels of government, of course, is running the city hall."

January 23, 2004 Washington, D.C.

★ ★ ★ ★

"A free, peaceful Zimbabwe has got the capacity to deliver a lot of goods and services which are needed on this continent in order to help aleve suffering."

July 9, 2003 *A classic Bush conjunction: in this case combining relieve and alleviate. Now it becomes clear what the Bayer Pharmaceuticals Corporation was thinking.* Pretoria, South Africa.

★ ★ ★ ★

PRESIDENTIAL SPEAK

"But the Congress giveth, the Congress taketh away. And these tax relief will be—will expire on an irregular basis."

February 19, 2004 Speaking in Washington, D.C.

★ ★ ★ ★

"It's hard to be a manufacturer in the state of Pennsylvania if you're worried about where your next energy is coming from."

March 15, 2003 Speaking in Ardmore, Pennsylvania.

★ ★ ★ ★

"Overwhelmingly, yet carefully targeted air strikes left entire enemy divisions without armor and without organization."

April 16, 2003 *The usual misalignment.* St. Louis, Missouri.

The Very Curious Language of George W. Bush™
Volume 3

PRESIDENTIAL SPEAK

"And, as you notice, yesterday one fellow tried to—was done in as, uh, he tried to conduct a suicide mission. In other words, an Iraqi policeman did their job."

October 28, 2003 *An policeman can be your friend.* The White House, Washington, D.C.

"...sometimes when you don't measure, you just shuffle kids through. Then you wake up at the high school level and find out that the illiteracy level of our children are appalling."

January 23, 2004 *Appalling, is right. – Editor.* Speaking in Washington, D.C.

PRESIDENTIAL SPEAK

"It's in the interest of—uh—uhh, long-term peace in the world that we—uhh—work for a free and secure and peaceful Iraq. A peeance, freeance secure Iraq in the midst of the Middle East will have enormous historical impact."

October 27, 2003 Perhaps 'peaceful' and 'free' were intended – but 'peeance' and 'freeance' were really what the President uttered on that October day.

"If an insurance carrier can spread risk across a variety of people or a variety of firms, it makes it more likely his health care goes down."

March 16, 2004 Speaking in Washington, D.C.

PRESIDENTIAL SPEAK

"Wait for us to succeed peace."

June 15, 2003 *I'm not sure how long we'll be waiting, because I'm just not sure — Editor.* Kennebunkport, Maine.

"The Oval Office is an interesting place to meet, particularly people who are beginning to struggle with democracy and freedom because it's a reminder that the institutions, at least in this country, are always bigger than the people. Sometimes we've got an all-right president, sometimes not all right. But the presidency, itself, exists."

January 22, 2004 *Might we hope, perchance, to do better than an 'all-right president'?* Roswell, New Mexico.

"What's it like when you come here? It's like being in a place with people who are willing to stand up to values that are important in this country."

March 8, 2004 *I stood up to my values once and was beaten back — Editor.* Dallas, Texas.

"And a free Iraq in the heart of the Middle East will make it more easy for us to not only secure America and other free nations, but will make it easier for there to be peace in the long run."

September 11, 2003 Washington, D.C.

"Home ownership is at the highest rate ever. That means there's more people ever in our history are able to say, 'I own something. I own my own home.' I went to Pearl's home and it was pretty special. Really special, wasn't it? She said, 'This is my home.' When I walked up the stairs, she didn't say this is anybody else's home, but her home. She said, 'Would you come into my home, please?'"

March 15, 2004 *Not one of the more stirring endorsements for home ownership.* Ardmore, Pennsylvania.

PRESIDENTIALSPEAK

"See, our job as policy people and members of Congress, have got to fix problems when we see them— they don't ignore problems, they don't hope the problems go away."

August 11, 2003 Summerhaven, Arizona.

★ ★ ★ ★

"We're, uhh, conscience of, uh, of uh, folks flying—you know, getting lists of people flying into our country and matching them now with a much improved database."

July 30, 2003 *Very, very close.* The White House, Washington, D.C.

★ ★ ★ ★

"There's a lot of initiatives around from the faith-based program that track the child who needs to be mentored. And the best place to find mentors, of course, is you can find them every Sunday."

July 16, 2003 *Continuing to single-handedly destroy the concept of tense agreement. Washington, D.C.*

"Heck, we're five percent of the world's population, which means there's 95 percent of the people ready for products that say, 'Made in the USA'."

March 16, 2004 *People of the world, consider yourselves warned. Washington, D.C.*

PRESIDENTIAL SPEAK

"And, anyway, no, listen, let me speak specifically to Nigeria. I have got good relations with President Obasanjo. Every time we have visited it has been a very cordial, up-front way."

July 3, 2003 Speaking in Washington, D.C.

"The other issue regarding health care is whether or not health care is affordable and available. And one reason it's not in certain communities is because there is too many lawsuits."

June 19, 2003 *There is too many lawsuits. No argument here.* Fridley, Minnesota.

PRESIDENTIAL SPEAK

"For years the freedom of our people were really never in doubt."

February 14, 2003 *I'm beginning to read and reread these to check myself. It's all beginning to sound perfectly OK – Editor.* Speaking at FBI headquarters, Washington, D.C.

★ ★ ★ ★

"There's two things I want to share with you on that. One, there's nothing better than a society which encourages people to own something, isn't there? Either to own your own business—how about the fact that this is a fellow who is born in El Salvador, comes here to our country, and now owns his own home? Isn't that one of the spectacular aspects?"

March 11, 2004 Bay Shore, New York.

PRESIDENTIAL SPEAK

"I appreciate Charlie Curie here. He's the administration of the Substance Abuse and Mental Health Services of the Department of Health and Human Services."

March 3, 2004 *All by himself?* Los Angeles, California.

★ ★ ★ ★

"See, one of the interesting things in the Oval Office—I love to bring people into the Oval Office—right around the corner from here—and say, this is where I office."

February 18, 2004 *Not sure how to comment – Editor.* Washington, D.C.

★ ★ ★ ★

PRESIDENTIAL SPEAK

"Earlier today, the Libyan government released Fathi Jahmi. She's a local government official who was imprisoned in 2002 for advocating free speech and democracy."

March 12, 2004 Paying tribute to Fathi Jahmi – a man – during a speech to commemorate International Women's Week. Washington, D.C.

"A lot of times, this country talks about our strengths, and we should. We talk about the military strength of America, and that's important. And we're going to keep us strong."

February 9, 2004 *OK.* Springfield, Missouri.

PRESIDENTIAL SPEAK

"Recession means that people's incomes, at the employer level, are going down. Basically, relative to costs, people are getting laid off."

February 19, 2004 *There's that Harvard MBA coming into play again. Washington, D.C.*

"I will continue to speak as clearly as I can that an attack on the Iraqi infrastructure by the Baathist is an attack on the Iraqi people. And it's those Iraqis are causing the continued suffering, where there's suffering in Iraq."

July 12, 2003 *Speaking as clearly as he can in Abuja, Nigera.*

PRESIDENTIAL SPEAK

"I want to thank you all for coming today to give me a chance to spell out a practical way to make life a more hopeful place for America and small business owners."

February 19, 2004 Sharing a curious view of life in Washington, D.C.

Bush: "Now, Judy is the co-founder of Genesis—is that an accurate statement?"
Judy Memberg: "Yes, it is."
Bush: "She's a social entrepreneur."
Judy Memberg: "I've never been called that, but okay."
Bush: "It's a plus."

March 15, 2004 Giving assurance to Judy Memberg. Ardmore, Pennsylvania.

PRESIDENTIAL✺SPEAK

"And we began to recover from the attacks on September the 11th because we're a strong people. We're resilient because there's an ownership society, a culture of ownership in America."

March 4, 2004 *We're resilient and strong because we own things? Is that how it works?* Bakersfield, California.

★ ★ ★ ★

"The March to War hurt the economy. Laura reminded me awhile ago that remember what was on the TV screens—she calls me, 'George W.', 'George W'. I call her "First Lady". No, anyway—she said, we said, March to War on our TV screen."

March 11, 2004 Bay Shore, New York.

PRESIDENTIAL SPEAK

"A small business owner's outlook is improved when there's a new product available that says, gosh, I'm meeting the needs of my employees and also being able to better control costs."

March 16, 2004 Washington, D.C.

"That's what we're here to discuss. It's an economic lesson. But we're not using Ph.D.s. Well, we're using Ph.D.s in the sense that we're talking to entrepreneurs who are on the front lines of making capital decisions every day."

March 16, 2004 Washington, D.C.

The Very Curious Language of George W. Bush™
Volume 3

2005 Desk Calendar of Presidential (Mis)Speak

Completely Updated
★ All New Quotes ★

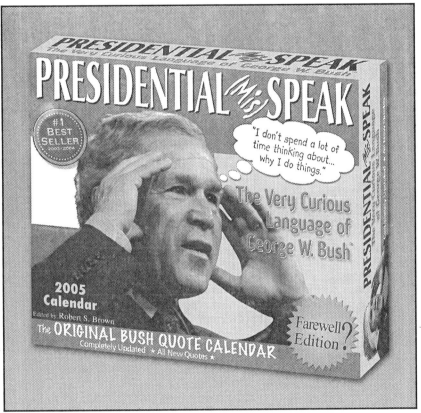

Available wherever books and calendars are sold
and at
www.bushcalendar.com

Skaneateles, New York